A picture book of Niagara Falls

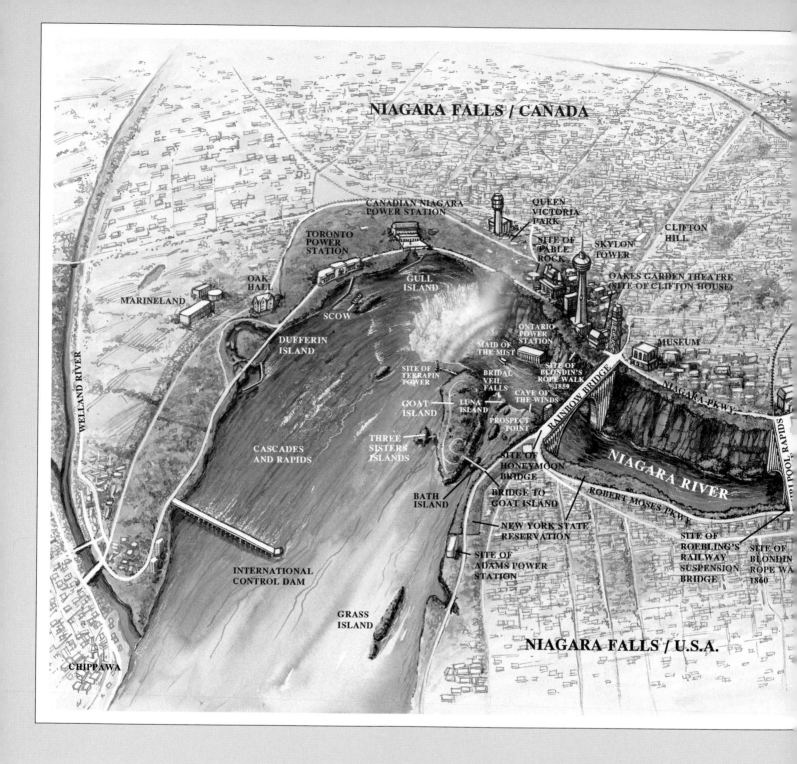

NIAGARA FALLS / CANADA

NIAGARA FALLS / U.S.A.

CANADIAN NIAGARA POWER STATION

QUEEN VICTORIA PARK

SITE OF TABLE ROCK

CLIFTON HILL

SKYLON TOWER

OAKES GARDEN THEATRE (SITE OF CLIFTON HOUSE)

TORONTO POWER STATION

GULL ISLAND

OAK HALL

MARINELAND

SCOW

ONTARIO POWER STATION

MUSEUM

DUFFERIN ISLAND

MAID OF THE MIST

SITE OF BLONDIN'S ROPE WALK 1859

SITE OF TERRAPIN TOWER

BRIDAL VEIL FALLS

CAVE OF THE WINDS

GOAT ISLAND

LUNA ISLAND

RAINBOW BRIDGE

NIAGARA PKWY

PROSPECT POINT

NIAGARA RIVER

WHIRLPOOL RAPIDS

CASCADES AND RAPIDS

THREE SISTERS ISLANDS

SITE OF HONEYMOON BRIDGE

ROBERT MOSES PKWY

WELLAND RIVER

BATH ISLAND

BRIDGE TO GOAT ISLAND

SITE OF ROEBLING'S RAILWAY SUSPENSION BRIDGE

SITE OF BLONDIN ROPE WA

NEW YORK STATE RESERVATION

INTERNATIONAL CONTROL DAM

SITE OF ADAMS POWER STATION

GRASS ISLAND

CHIPPAWA

*...this
prodigious
cadence
of
water...*

FATHER LOUIS HENNEPIN
1697

Niagara Falls
Thomas Chambers
oil on canvas
c. 1832-40

A PICTURE BOOK
of Niagara Falls

WRITTEN AND EDITED BY
Pierre Berton

DESIGN: Frank Newfeld RESEARCH: Barbara Sears COLOUR PHOTOGRAPHY: Paul Casselman

M&S

Canadian Cataloguing in Publication Data

Berton, Pierre, 1920 –
    Pierre Berton's picture book of Niagara Falls

ISBN 0-7710-1214-4
1. Niagara Falls (N.Y. and Ont.) - Pictorial works.
2. Niagara Falls (N.Y. and Ont.) - History.
I. Title.
FC3095.N5B37 1993   917.13'39   C93-093900-X
F127.N8B37 1993

PRINTED AND BOUND IN CANADA
BY METROPOLE LITHO, MONTREAL

MAP: Douglas Donald

DESIGN:

© Frank Newfeld Studio

McClelland & Stewart Inc.
The Canadian Publishers
481 University Avenue
Toronto, Ontario
M5G 2E9

DISTRIBUTED IN THE U.S. BY
ST. MARTIN'S PRESS, NEW YORK

ARCHIVAL PICTURE CREDITS
AIC/Art Institute of Chicago
BECHS/Buffalo and Erie County
    Historical Society
BEN/Buffalo *Evening News*
CGA/Corcoran Gallery of Art
CP/Canapress
FN/Frank Newfeld
GEH/George Eastman House
HCL/Harvard College Library
HM/Heckscher Museum
HPC/Hulton Picture Company
HRHRCUT/Harry Ransom Humanities
    Research Center, University of Texas
HS/Hamilton *Spectator*
ISG/Ira Spanierman Gallery
JJGC/Jo Ann and Julian Ganz Collection
LC/Library of Congress

LHDNFNY/Local History Department,
    Niagara Falls, New York, Public Library
MB/Michael Bailey
MFAB/Museum of Fine Arts, Boston
MM/McCord Museum
MOMA/Museum of Modern Art
MTPL/Metropolitan Toronto Public Library
NAO/National Archives, Ottawa
NB/Nabisco Brands
NFOPL/Niagara Falls, Ontario, Public
    Library
NGAW/National Gallery of Art,
    Washington
NGO/National Gallery, Ottawa
NMAASI/National Museum of American
    Art, Smithsonian Institution
NMPC/Niagara Mohawk Power Corp.

NPC/Niagara Parks Commission
NPGL/National Portrait Gallery, London
NYHS/New York Historical Society
NYPA/New York Power Authority
OA/Ontario Archives
OH/Ontario Hydro
RPIAC/Rensselaer Polytechnic Institute
    Archives Collection
SI/Smithsonian Institution
SPNEA/Society for the Preservation of
    New England Antiquities
SUCB/State University College, Buffalo
TS/*Toronto Star*
WA/Wadsworth Atheneum
WH/Wes Hill
YUTTA/York University Toronto
    Telegram Archives

p 4/5, Thomas Chambers, *Niagara Falls*, c. 1832-40, oil, WA, Ella Gallup Sumner and Mary Catlin Sumner Collection

THE LURE OF THE FALLS
pp.18/19, MTPL, hand coloured by Frank Newfeld; 20, left, NPGL; 20, right LC; 21, left, HRHRCUT; 21, right, LC; 22, left and right, LC; 23, left, NPGL; 23, right, MOMA; 24, Thomas Davies, *Niagara Falls from Below,* watercolour, c. 1762-68, NYHS; 25, top, attributed to John Vander Lyn, *A View of Niagara Falls*, 1801, oil/canvas, SPNEA, Codman House Collection, photograph by David Bohl; 25, Minott, *Niagara Falls*, oil, canvas, 1818, NYHS; 26, top, George Catlin, *Bird's-Eye View of Niagara*, 1821, BECHS; 26/7, bottom, George Catlin, *Niagara Falls*, 1827-28, NMAASI, gift of Mrs. Joseph Harrison, Jr; 27, George Catlin, *Portage Around the Falls at Niagara at Table Rock*, 1847-48, oil/canvas, © NGAW, Paul Mellon Collection; 28/9, Frederic Church, *Niagara*, 1857, oil/canvas, CGA; 30, top, Jasper Francis Cropsey, *Niagara Falls*, 1860, oil/canvas, JJGC; 30, bottom, Jasper Francis Cropsey, *Niagara Falls in Winter*, 1868, oil/canvas, photograph © 1992, AIC; all rights reserved; 31, Albert Bierstadt, *Waterfall and Rainbow*, c. 1870s, ISG; 32, John Henry Twachtman, *Niagara Falls*, c. 1894, oil/canvas, gift of John Gellatly, NMAASI; 33, LHDNFNY; 34, LC; 35, top, MM; 35, bottom, NGO; 36, HPC; 37 GEH; 38 MM; 39, LC; 40, LC; 41 NAO, PA-181102; 44, NAO, PA-143218; 45, LC; 47, top, BECHS; 52, top, NAO, PA-148630; 52, bottom, NPC

THE FALLS: THEN AND NOW
pp. 65, top, William James Bennett, *Niagara Falls from the American Side,* NAO, C-42248; 66, top, BECHS; 66, bottom, HPC; 67, William James Bennett, *Niagara Falls...from Under Table Rock,* NAO, C-41027; 68, James Pattison Cockburn, *The Falls of Niagara,* NAO, C-40984; 69, top, MTPL; 69, bottom left, HPC; 69, bottom right, LC; 70, top, Augustus Köllner, *American Falls,* NAO, C-13434; 70, bottom, Augustus Köllner, *The Rapids at Niagara,* NAO, C-42283; 71, Ferdinand Richardt, *Niagara Falls,* c. 1855, oil/canvas, HM; 74, NAO, PA-103132; 74/5, Robert Reginald Whale, *The Canada Southern Railway at Niagara Falls,* c. 1870, oil/canvas, NGO; 76, top, RPIAC; 76, bottom, HPC; 77, anon, *The Railway Suspension Bridge Over Niagara Falls,* U.S., c. 1855, oil/canvas, M.M. Karolik Collection, MFAB, 77, bottom, NYHS; 78, top, BECHS; 78, bottom, LHDNFNY; 79, top and middle, LHDNFNY; 79, bottom, LC; 80 top, HPC; 80, bottom, SI; 82, left, MTPL; 82, centre, BECHS; 82, right, OH; 83, left, NYPA; 83, right, SI; 84/5, SI; 86/7, SI; 88, SI; 89, top, MTPL; 89, bottom, OH; 90, OH; 91 NYPA; 92/3, BECHS; 96, OH.

THE DRAMA OF THE FALLS
pp. 114/15, HPC; 115, HPC; 116, left, NYHS; 117, left, HCL; 117, right, OA, hand coloured by Frank Newfeld; 118, LHDNFNY; 119, top right, NAO, PA-181218; 119, bottom left, BECHS; 119, bottom right, LC; 120, top, BECHS; 120, bottom, LHDNFNY; 121, top, BECHS; 121, bottom left, drawing, FN; 121, bottom right, GEH; 122, bottom, LC; 123, LHDNFNY; 124, BECHS; 125, LHDNFNY; 126, top, BEN; 127, CP; 128, top left, SUCB; 128, top right, MB; 128, bottom, YUTTA; 130, bottom, NPC; 131, top, HS; 131, bottom left, LHDNFNY; 131, bottom right, LC; 132, top, NB; 132, bottom, LHDNFNY; 133, NPC; 134/5, BECHS; 136, NPC; 137, top and bottom, BECHS; 138, BECHS; 139, NFOPL; 139, BECHS; 140, WH; 140/1, YUTTA; 142/3, SUCB; 143, TS; 144, NYPA; 145, NAO, C-77893; 146, NPC; 147, LC; 148, LC; 149, LC; 150, top left, LC; 150, top right, LHDNFNY; 151, NPC.

Contents

Reflections in the mists

"Something changed the way people looked at the Falls, and that something was a new way of looking at Nature."

NOBODY, IT SEEMS, CAN RESIST THE LURE OF Niagara Falls. Almost all visitors to North America, be they Japanese or Italian, Korean or Spanish, come with plans already made to see the Falls as soon as possible after the plane lands. Twelve million people arrive every summer to gaze on these sparkling green waters. Even would-be suicides, who might make an easier exit at home with a handy revolver, noose, or cyanide capsule, insist on seeing the sights before committing themselves to the fury below.

John Lazarus, a stocky sixty-year-old from Mount Carmel, Pennsylvania, was one of these. In 1900 he planned his suicide as carefully as others planned their honeymoons. He bought a one-way ticket to Niagara, took his time, saw the sights (hiring a hack to get to all points of interest), paid for a ride on the electric trolley that travelled the Great Gorge Route, and strolled through the sylvan forests of Goat Island before leaping to his death. See Niagara and die. For Lazarus, as for so many others (and for so many reasons), it was the place to be. It still is, as the pictures in this book show.

Although Victoria Falls, hidden in Africa's dark heart, are higher and wider, it is the Falls of Niagara that have become the metaphor for excess. We speak of a Niagara of words pouring from a politician's mouth, a Niagara of good wishes, a Niagara of paper, a Niagara of gold.

To the world, this immense cataract, once concealed in the wild interior of an unknown continent, has become a familiar. Is there a human being left who has not made a nodding acquaintance with its image? Millions of picture postcards and family snapshots, not to mention tourist brochures, salon photos, paintings, engravings, and films–a veritable Niagara, indeed–have made this natural wonder almost commonplace. Yet to those who hang over the balustrade at Queen Victoria Park, with the roar in their ears and the spray in their faces, it can only seem extraordinary. Who can resist the spectacle? Every second the equivalent of half a million bathtubs of water tumbles over a precipice twenty storeys high.

Once the Falls were seen as a Gothic horror. In 1683, Father Hennepin, the first man to describe the cataract in print, called it "frightful" and said he could not "behold it without a shudder." Midway through the next century, the Swedish naturalist Pehr Kalm said it made his hair stand on end. In 1805, the naturalist-poet Alexander Wilson said the Falls "seized, at once, all power of speech away and filled our souls with terror and dismay."

By the 1830s, when the Fashionable Tour was bringing the upper classes from the steamy cities of the American South to the cooler environs of New England, upstate New York, and Canada, the cataract had ceased to terrify. Harriet Beecher, the future author of *Uncle Tom's Cabin*, was enraptured. "Oh, it is lovelier than it is great," she exulted. Charles Dickens saw "nothing of gloom or terror" but only an "Image of Beauty." Anna Jameson, the British art critic, who at first in 1836 confessed herself disappointed, changed her mind after long contemplation and decided that nobody had ever done justice to the Falls' "inexpressible, inconceivable beauty."

Something was happening to change the way people saw the Falls, and that something was a new way of looking at nature. For centuries, nature had usually been an encumbrance. The great cataract in particular had been a monumental nuisance for the native peoples and early explorers, involving a long and exhausting portage. But the poets of the Romantic Era changed attitudes. From the English Lake District to the isles of Greece, nature had become a kind of religion: in Wordsworth's words, "a presence that disturbs me with the joy of elevated thoughts."

That coincided with the arrival of the railways in the mid-1830s–a development that soon placed the Falls within reach of ordinary people. The wedding journey of the wealthy, in which a gaggle of relatives travelled with the nuptial couple to a fashionable spa, was replaced by the more private and more romantic honeymoon. Niagara was easily accessible; comfortable accommodation already existed; and there was something to see. The Falls ceased to be a resort for the upper classes. It was on the way to becoming a carnival for the masses.

The carnival had begun as early as 1827, when three tavernkeepers arranged to send a derelict ship, the *Michigan*, over the Falls with a cargo of live animals. Two years later, the first of the daredevils, Sam Patch, the Jersey Jumper, took his life in his hands by leaping (successfully) from the Goat Island cliff into the churning waters below.

Ever since the days when Greeks attempted the Hellespont, men and women have tested themselves by tackling natural obstacles. The Horseshoe Falls were irresistible. Yet there is no objective reason to go over the great cataract in a barrel or to cross the gorge on a tightrope–nothing to be gained for the good of mankind, no new worlds to open up, no mysterious secrets to unlock. The funambulists and the barrel plungers had less exalted but more human reasons for risking their lives than those that motivated the men and women who tackled the great rivers of Africa or the frozen islands of the Arctic. It was fame and profit they sought. (The first came quickly; the second was more elusive.) They fitted easily into the great age of hype with which the name of Phineas T. Barnum is irrevocably linked.

"The Railway era transformed the Falls.
A new word, tourism, *entered the language."*

THE GREAT CATARACT REFLECTS THE FADS AS IT reflects the concerns of each generation. The Darwinian revolution was preceded by the geological revolution, whose protagonist was Charles Lyell, the scientist who scrambled up Niagara's cliffs to prove the earth far older than the Biblical scholars had reckoned. Long before the Falls of the Niagara began to gnaw a canyon upriver toward Lake Erie, a prehistoric watercourse had flowed northwest in the same general area. Lyell even found a section of that ancient stream buried in the glacial rubble northwest of the Whirlpool. He figured the age of the Falls as 35,000 years; modern discoveries have reduced it to 12,500. Thus the presence of the Falls challenged the dictum of those creationists who insisted that the earth was no more than 5,000 years old.

Niagara Falls can boast a succession of firsts, each of which mirrors the times: the first museum in North America; the first railway suspension bridge in the world; the first use of public money to expropriate land for public parks; the first hydro-electric power development in history.

Thomas Barnett, an obsessive collector and hotel-keeper, started the first museum near Table Rock. It still exists, albeit in a newer building, with Barnett's eclectic collection intact. Barnett collected everything, including his own dog, an animal with no hind legs whose stuffed body, as well as its skeleton, is still on display.

As his collection grew, Barnett faced a cash-flow crisis. This was abetted by his continuing feud with his competitor, Saul Davis, who ran the Table Rock Hotel, better known in the 1860s as the Cave of the Forty Thieves. In this age of the confidence man, Davis's con was typical of the times. He promised tourists free photographs and free passage down his private stairway to view the Falls from the base. Of course, nothing was free, and those who refused to pay the outrageous prices faced a beating at the hands of Davis's thugs.

As for Barnett, he tried to recoup his fortunes by staging a buffalo hunt at the Falls with none other than Wild Bill Hickok in charge. The tawdry attempt to reproduce the old West was a dismal failure, and Barnett lost his museum in a bankruptcy sale. By the bitterest of ironies, the buyer was his old enemy, Saul Davis.

By the early 1870s, when Barnett staged his Wild West buffalo hunt, Niagara Falls, Ontario, had become a hell-raising community. The famous "Front," a strip on the gorge's rim no more than three hundred yards wide, stretched a quarter of a mile from the Falls to the Clifton House. For half a century it provided a haven for every kind of huckster, gambler, barker, confidence man, and swindler. Here half a dozen hotels and a hodgepodge of shops, booths, taverns, and "Indian" souvenir tents were all jammed together. Hack drivers shouted for fares; itinerant photographers plied their trade; roguish Irish girls flirted with the souvenir hunters.

The railway era transformed the Falls. A new word, "tourism," entered the language. Gone were the days when the moneyed class arrived to stay for several months. Cheaper fares and fast trains made it possible for an ordinary couple to enjoy a one-day trip to the great cataract without putting up at one of the big hotels that lined the gorge.

The tourist era began after John Roebling built his railway suspension bridge–the wonder of the age– across the gorge. Nothing like it had ever been constructed before. Critics scoffed, but Roebling's bridge did not fall down. The trains ran, the masses arrived, and the carnival flourished.

But Niagara was falling into disrepute, suffering from what one journalist called "the disastrous effects of a bad name." If the Canadian side was dominated by barkers and swindlers, the American bank was disfigured by ugly stone dams, gristmills, outdoor clotheslines, heaps of sawdust, stables, advertising placards, shanties, lumberyards, a pulp mill, and a gasworks. Greed predominated, represented by "the very pick of the touts and rascals of the world," in the words of the English designer William Morris. On the

Canadian side at least, you could actually view the Falls. But on the American side, every vantage point was fenced in so that there was no place from which the falling water could be seen without payment.

It was these excesses that finally persuaded a group of high-minded citizens to launch a campaign to preserve the Falls. Preservation movements are common in our day, but in the 1880s the idea of setting aside a tract of untrammelled wilderness in perpetuity for future generations to admire and enjoy was a novel one. Few North Americans cared or even thought about the continent's natural beauty. The emphasis was on "progress," which meant carving out roadways, draining swamps, clearing forests, and exploiting natural wonders, such as the Falls, for profit. Those who subdued the wilderness were seen not as vandals but as nation builders.

The fight to save the environment of the Falls was staged by two groups of people, each working on one side of the international border. It lasted for fifteen years—a long, exhausting struggle that started slowly but would eventually involve the leading figures of the day, including a number of politicians who had no stomach for the principle of public ownership of natural attractions.

On the American side, the preservation movement preoccupied such major figures as Frederic Church, the painter (see pp. 28-29), Frederick Law Olmsted, the creator of New York's Central Park, and the young architect Henry Hobson Richardson, whose interpretation of the Romanesque style would soon sweep the continent. (Toronto's Old City Hall is a good example of Richardsonian Romanesque).

The preservationists on both sides were aided by the Governor General of Canada, the elegant Lord Dufferin, who, in a meeting with the Governor of New York in 1873, urged that the state and the province of Ontario buy up the lands and buildings around the Falls to form a small international public park. That happy concept never came to fruition, but the campaign persisted on both sides of the border. New York got its Reservation in 1885; never before had a state of the Union used public money to expropriate property for such a purpose. Thanks to a royal commission headed by a brilliant émigré, Casimir Gzowski, Canada was able to follow suit two years later. Queen Victoria Park became the first provincially owned park in Ontario. Today, after considerable expansion, the green belt stretches from the foot of the Falls to Lake Ontario.

"The movement to harness the Falls dovetailed neatly with the Great Age of Heroic Invention."

SINCE THE DAY MORE THAN THREE CENTURIES ago when Father Hennepin became the first European traveller to write about the Falls, mankind has not been able to keeps its hands off the great cataract. It was not possible to let it stand by itself—a glittering curtain of water surrounded by a brooding forest. It had to be *used.* Thus it became a backdrop for vaudeville acts, a mecca for thrill seekers, a headquarters for entrepreneurs, and a power source for the burgeoning industrial heartland of southwestern Ontario and upstate New York.

The movement to harness the Falls for hydro-electric power dovetailed neatly with another historical period—the Great Age of Heroic Invention, as it has

been called. In the fading years of the nineteenth century, a single experimenter, working in the family woodshed, could still make a revolutionary discovery. In just such a woodshed in 1884, a young college graduate, Charles Martin Hall, found a way to separate aluminum from common clay. Hard on the heels of that discovery, a self-taught chemical wizard, Edward Goodrich Acheson, found a way to produce a new abrasive. He called it Carborundum. Next to diamond dust, it was the hardest ever known.

Between inventors like Hall and Acheson and the great cataract, there developed a symbiotic relationship. Both men moved their manufacturing operations to Niagara Falls, New York, to make the best use of the immense reservoir of power locked up in those tumbling waters. Thus, the American community lived up to its original name of Manchester by becoming a blue-collar factory town, while Niagara Falls, Ontario, became a tourist mecca. For it was the Canadian Falls, being the more spectacular of the two cataracts, that lured the visitors.

The Americans were the first to exploit the Falls' power in a big way. For centuries running water had been used to operate gristmills. As early as 1758, the French had used the rapids above the cataract to turn mill wheels. But it was not until 1889 that a serious attempt was made to harness the vast potential of the waterfall.

It is a remarkable story. Electrical power was then in its infancy. Thomas Edison had just developed the first incandescent light bulb, using direct current. But no one knew exactly how the force of the Falls should be used to turn wheels. And no one knew whether or not electrical power could be transmitted over long distances.

The men who formed the Niagara Falls Power Company and its sister firm, the Cataract Construction Company, took an enormous gamble. They proceeded to build a vast tailrace tunnel directly under the American town to draw off water from a point above the Falls, without being sure how the power from that source would be distributed. They simply assumed that sooner or later the problem would be solved. And it was.

There was a time when more than one scientist was perfectly prepared to obliterate the Falls in favour of massive power. The great Lord Kelvin himself echoed the hopes of the electrical industry when he stated baldly in 1897, "I do not hope that our children's children will ever see Niagara's cataract." A compromise between the advocates of natural beauty and those of raw energy saved the Falls. Thanks to an international agreement, half the water that would normally pour over the Falls is now diverted by conduits and tunnels to the two Sir Adam Beck hydro-electric stations on the Canadian side and to the Robert Moses Niagara Power Plant on the American. In winter, when only a few tourists arrive, the Niagara's flow is cut in half again. The sheet of water is thinner, but few notice the difference.

"Niagara's mighty forces could benefit the world not only materially but also morally."

EVER SINCE THE FIRST WHITE EXPLORERS BURST out of the wintry woods to view the noble cataract, there has been a transcendental quality to the Falls. Father Hennepin, who carried a portable altar strapped to his back, is said to have dropped to his knees to do obeisance to his Maker, his ears assailed as if by divine thunder. The young Nathaniel Hawthorne described himself as a pilgrim approaching a shrine. Caroline Gilman, the Boston-born author and poet, said she "felt the moral influence of the scene acting on my spiritual nature." She was one of many who saw in the cataract the manifestation of the Creator's design. To William Henry Bartlett, the artist, to see Niagara was "to see God in the excellence of His power." Charles Dickens felt "how near to my Creator I was standing."

This view of the Falls as the moral and inspirational centre of the continent appealed to those Utopian dreamers who, at the end of the nineteenth century, had their own grandiose plans for the Falls. The most ambitious of these was King Camp Gillette, who later went on to invent the safety razor and who, like so many others, was caught up in the wave of optimism that accompanied the dawn of the electrical age. Nature at her most awesome had been subdued. Niagara's mighty forces could benefit the world not only materially but also morally. Electricity as energy was clean and pure, a symbol of peace and harmony in contrast to coal, grimy and corrupt, hidden in the murky bowels of the earth. The World's Columbian Exposition of 1893–the famous "White City"– lit entirely by electricity, pointed the way to Utopia.

Gillette's concept was the most grandiose. His community, centring around the Falls, would not be just another city; thanks to Niagara's unlimited power it would be the *only* city in the United States. Gillette had a vision of 24,000 gigantic apartment buildings, each twenty-four storeys high, and each accommodating 2,500 tenants "free from the annoyance of housekeeping." Designed as a vast rectangle, 135 miles long by 45 miles wide, the city would be built on a three-level platform one hundred feet in depth, covering the entire countryside. It did not seem to bother Gillette that the Falls themselves–the very reason for his dream city–would be hidden.

Utopias such as these were mere fantasies. It took a quirky health faddist named Henry Perky to realize his own dream and build the world's most modern factory within view of the Falls. Perky, the inventor of Shredded Wheat, chose the Falls because that was where the customers were. In an era when most workplaces were dark, stuffy, and airless, he erected the factory of the future, "a temple of cleanliness," its 30,000 panes of glass making it "the cleanest, finest, most hygienic factory in the world." One hundred thousand visitors tramped through it annually, all potential consumers who could help put Shredded Wheat on the map.

Perky's successful scheme to use the Falls as a backdrop for his "Temple of Nutrition" has had its modern counterparts. After the Second World War, the site was one of three seriously considered as headquarters for the United Nations. Niagara lost out to New York, but the idea of using the cataract as a symbol for peace and harmony never died. In the spring of 1992, the Canadian stage magician Doug Henning announced that he and the Maharishi Mahesh Yogi would construct a transcendental theme park at the Falls, a kind of carnival shrine to the Yogi's particular form of franchised meditation.

Utopia, of course, has its dark side. The Falls have become architects of their own pollution. Had it not been for the power released by the cataract, manufacturers dependent on electricity would not have arrived to foul the air and the waters of Niagara. The electro-chemical industries of the American city thrive on Falls power, but the by-product of that power has been industrial waste. Some of that devil's brew surfaced in the 1970s, sparking a citizens' revolt that successfully fought city hall and caused the abandonment of an entire community. Today the words "Love Canal" symbolize a growing concern for the environment that has become one of the great crusades of the late twentieth century.

*"The twin communities that
feed off the Falls are as different
as steel and silk."*

THE TWIN COMMUNITIES THAT FACE EACH OTHER across the Niagara River both feed off the Falls, yet they are as different as steel and silk. Niagara Falls, New York, remains a city of factory workers. Niagara Falls, Ontario, is all glitz and showmanship. Until 1992, the largest Ferris wheel in the world sat on the Canadian side in the heart of the Clifton Hill carnival. On the American side lies Buffalo Avenue, a smoky boulevard of chemical factories. Canada draws the fun seekers–and always has–because the Horseshoe Falls are a far bigger attraction than their American counterpart, an anomaly that disturbed and distressed some leading American expansionists in the era of Manifest Destiny.

Visitors to the Falls on both sides of the gorge arrive expecting to be entertained. Unlike the early travellers, who scrambled down the cliffside through a rubble of intertwined boulders and roots, modern travellers take stairs and elevators to the old Cave of the Winds on the American side or to the tunnels drilled into the rock behind the sheet of water on the Canadian. Shielded from the spray by yellow slickers imported from Japan, they can experience the original thrills without the danger and exertion. The newest *Maid of the Mist* takes them to within a few hundred feet of the thundering Horseshoe; the Spanish Aero Car suspends them over the maelstrom of the Whirlpool.

Along the neon length of Clifton Hill on the Canadian side, visitors are reminded constantly of the daredevils who helped make the Falls notorious and who enliven these pages. There are barrels everywhere: miniature barrels for those who want a photo of themselves tumbling over a painted cataract; historical barrels, in which the impetuous and foolhardy met their fate; and counterfeit barrels, such as the replica Annie Taylor had made to stand in for the one that was stolen from her.

Annie was the first over the Falls. Others have followed in her wake. Surprisingly, most have survived. Yet it is death, or its imminence, that has always preoccupied those who come to goggle at the cataract. When the great Blondin glided across the gorge on his tightrope, he frustrated an audience that expected to see him fall to his doom. As the Niagara Falls *Gazette* reported ghoulishly, "everybody is disappointed to see him display such agility and courage."

Blondin was immovable. Invited to push him off his rope, Harry Colcord, his manager, heaved, shoved, and sweated to no avail. Blondin stood firm. Indeed, no rope walker ever met his end over Niagara, unless one counts the unlucky Stephen Peer, an assistant to Signor Bellini, who, while drunk and wearing ordinary street shoes, tried to emulate his master and immediately fell to his death.

The astonishing feats of the rope walkers produced in the onlookers the same kind of Gothic chill that a good horror movie evokes. Ersatz thrills are to be found everywhere on the Canadian side. Castle Dracula and the Haunted House draw the tourists. In the IMAX production in a nearby theatre, the great feats of the past have been recreated on a screen so gigantic that the audience feels itself part of the action. These include the miraculous unplanned fall of seven-year-old Roger Woodward, who survived the force of the Horseshoe wearing nothing more than a pair of shorts and a life jacket.

The IMAX production has itself become part of the Falls legend. By recreating past thrills, the IMAX actors were themselves facing the kind of danger that threatened their historical counterparts. Roger Woodward's sister, Deanne, was plucked from the water just fifteen feet short of the crest of the Horseshoe. Significantly, no stuntwoman could be found who would attempt to recreate that feat. Jan Gordon, an amateur actress, was herself in peril in spite of wearing an underwater harness. But you cannot fake the Falls or build a replica of them in a studio backlot. She pulled the stunt off successfully and moved into the mythology.

That is part of the cataract's appeal: it is the real thing. Tourists may pose against a painted backdrop of the Falls as they sometimes did in the past. But no photograph, no painting, no film can ever reproduce the uncanny tingle that still runs up the spine of anyone who gazes upon that wall of foaming spray, never still, never silent, always luminous—noble, awesome, terrifying, beautiful, sublime. No wonder that the millions who stare into those rainbow-bedecked waters—kings and princes, presidents and poets, movie stars, painters, honeymooners, would-be suicides, and just plain people—seem hypnotized by their power and their glory. It is an experience that cannot be replicated. There is only one Niagara Falls.

The Lure of the Falls

Since the days of the early explorers, the Falls have become the mecca of North America. Poets and painters, princes, peasants, and plain people have been drawn to them, lured by their power and their glory, awed by their thunder, dazzled by their rainbows. Few other natural wonders have had such an effect on so many millions.

Europe's first vision of Niagara Falls

The first white man to describe Niagara Falls was a Recollet priest. Father Louis Hennepin was sent to Lake Erie by René-Robert Cavelier, Sieur de La Salle, to find a spot where that explorer might build a barque. The priest and his party arrived at the mouth of the Niagara River on December 6, 1678, and camped at the Falls two nights later. Hennepin's description of "this most dreadful Gulph," which he "could not behold without a shudder," imprinted on European minds an image of the Falls as a Gothic horror, hidden in the dark wilderness of the new continent. This hand-tinted drawing, showing mountains in the background, was engraved from Hennepin's description and shows an additional cascade, long since eroded away. Hennepin exaggerated the height of the Falls, making them 500 feet high instead of 170 but also narrower– rather like the more familiar mountain waterfalls in Europe. The engraving became the basis for all pictorial representations of the Falls for the next 60 years. Even as late as 1817, Hennepin's version, complete with distant mountains, was appearing on maps of the region.

From notable visitors:

Charles Dickens

Abraham Lincoln

"When I felt
how near to my Creator
I was standing, the first
effect, and the enduring one—
instant and lasting—
of the tremendous spectacle
was Peace. Peace of Mind:
Tranquillity: Calm
recollections of the Dead:
Great Thoughts of
Eternal Rest and Happiness:
Nothing of Gloom and Terror.
Niagara was at once stamped upon
my heart, an Image of Beauty. . ."

"The thing
that struck me most forcibly
when I saw the falls was
where in the world did
all that water come from?"

wit, praise, and cynicism

Harriet Beecher [later Stowe]

Mark Twain

"I felt as if
I could have gone over with
the waters; it would be so
beautiful a death;
there would be no fear in it,
I felt the rock tremble
with a sort of joy."

"You can descend
a staircase a hundred
and fifty feet down, and stand
at the edge of the water.
After you have done it,
you will wonder why
you did it; but
you will then be too late."

"A vast reiteration of falling water"

H.G. Wells

Oscar Wilde

"The real interest
of Niagara for me was not
in the waterfall, but in
the human accumulations
about it. They stood for
the future, threats and promises,
and the waterfall was
just a vast reiteration of
falling water. The note of
growth in human accomplishment
rose clear and triumphant
above the elemental thunder."

"When I first saw
the falls I was disappointed in
the outline.
Every American bride
is taken there, and the sight
must be one of the earliest,
if not the keenest, disappointments
in American married life."

or a "breeding place for . . . touts"?

Rupert Brooke

"Niagara
is the central home
and breeding place for all
the touts on earth. . .
who have no apparent object
in the world
but just purely, simply, merely,
indefatigably–to tout."

Marilyn Monroe

"The falls
produce a lot of electricity,
but the honeymooners
don't use very much of it
at night."

Through
the eyes of
the painter

Thomas Davies, Niagara Falls from Below, *circa 1766, watercolour*

Nearly one hundred established artists have been drawn to Niagara Falls, leaving behind a rich legacy that has added to our knowledge of the cataract as it once was and as it has changed over time. One of the earliest was Thomas Davies, whose painting above is the first known portrait of the Falls that can be called accurate. In his three views of the Falls, Davies, a military artist and trained watercolourist, helped to correct the exaggerations of Father Louis Hennepin, the explorer who visited the Falls a century earlier.

The sense of terror experienced by those who teetered on
the lip of Table Rock was caught by John Vander Lyn (ABOVE) in 1801
and in a more violent study by an artist known as Minott in 1818.

A painter-showman anticipates the art of aerial photography

George Catlin, famed for his studies of Plains Indians, was a showman as well as an artist. The remarkable painting on the right, made in 1827, almost a century before the era of aerial photography, shows how the Falls area looked in the days of early settlement. The savage wilderness, which excited so many artists, has been pushed back and replaced by neat orchards and ploughed fields, reaching upriver to Chippawa Creek. The village of Manchester (Niagara Falls, New York) can be seen emerging from the forest at left; the bridge to Goat Island is clearly delineated; new roads are shown in detail. The painting was created after Catlin made a scale model of the area, which he exhibited on both sides of the Atlantic to generous praise.

Catlin's model, from which this famous painting was made, charmed the London art critics, who praised it as "representing in perfect proportion, and colour, every house, tree, rock."

The inventive Catlin, having foreshadowed an aerial future, turned to the past to produce, in 1847, this illustration showing Father Hennepin and his Indian companions portaging around the Falls in January 1679.

Unable to squeeze the Falls into a conventional shape, Catlin adapted his canvas to fit his mile-long subject.

A breathtaking canvas stuns the art world

Of the hundreds of paintings made of Niagara Falls, this one, by common consent, is the greatest. The work of a brilliant landscape artist, Frederic Church, the gigantic canvas–seven and a half feet long–sold for the unheard of sum of $4,500 in 1857

and went on immediate display in New York. Later, in London, it drew gasps from the critics and public alike, who came by the thousands to view it. The age of photography has lessened the painting's impact, but to viewers in the mid-century, who seemed to be standing on the very brink of the precipice, it was "Niagara with the roar left out." Church boldly abandoned the conventional foreground in order to capture the great sweep of the Horseshoe from the water's edge, something no other artist had attempted.

Vivid colours from the palettes of two romantic painters

Jasper Francis Cropsey and Albert Bierstadt were among the leading landscape artists of the 1860s who followed Frederic Church to the Falls. Both painted with more intense colours than their predecessors, no doubt because of the influence of John Ruskin, the British art critic, who espoused the scintillating canvases of J.M.W. Turner.

Cropsey painted the sylvan scene at left in 1860, returning in 1868 to make the winter painting below. In one critic's words, the sun made the ice "look like a strange fairy sculpture."

Bierstadt (RIGHT), Church's great rival, was the first to make oil sketches out of doors. A master at handling light and mist, his work was luminous and his colours vivid but never garish.

By 1894, when this painting was made,
the camera had had a devastating effect
on realistic art. John Henry Twachtman's
study of the Horseshoe Falls shows the
influence of the Impressionist movement
in Europe. The academic artists took a
back seat to the so-called "modernists."

The camera takes over

Crouched over his bulky camera, an itinerant photographer prepares to shoot the Horseshoe Falls, *circa* 1865. Daguerreotypes went on sale at Niagara in the late 1840s, followed by ambrotypes and later tintypes. But it was the paper photograph, printed from a wet glass negative, that changed things. It also started the stereopticon craze of the Confederation years. The picture above was made in duplicate for 3-D viewing by a second "professor," as such men were known.

The first photograph of the Falls

This is the earliest photograph made of Niagara Falls. In 1839, when the daguerreotype was perfected, Noël-Marie Lerebours, a French optician, dispatched various cameramen to make pictures of the world's most famous sites. Transferred to engraving plates, these were published as a set of hand-coloured aquatint prints, including the one above by an amateur, H.L. Pattinson.

Platt D. Babbitt, renowned for his views of tourists at the Falls, enjoyed a monopoly at Prospect Point. It was from his kiosk (RIGHT) that the picture below was made. Babbitt placed his tourists closer to the lens–and to the water's edge– than the others did. Note the polished clarity of this brilliant daguerreotype made about 1853.

*William England, chief photographer for the London
Stereoscopic Company, made this view in 1859,
the year the great Blondin crossed the gorge on a tightrope.
His photographs of that event (SEE p.115) became
the company's all-time best-selling images.*

*Like many stereoscopic views of the time,
this one, also by England, was tinted by hand.
England invented the focal-plane shutter camera,
which greatly improved clarity and revolutionized
the art of photography. England died in 1896.*

Goat Island, in the days of the crinoline

The bridge to the Three Sisters islands

The Horseshoe Falls from Table Rock

William Notman

The three photographs on the left are from the studio of William Notman, a Scottish immigrant who became Canada's most celebrated nineteenth-century photographer. He and his 55 camera-men travelled the country making superlative landscape photographs. Notman himself was best known as a celebrity photo-grapher. Every notable who visited Montreal sat for his portrait camera.

William Henry Jackson

Like Notman, this American was one of the most prolific photographers of his day. And, like Notman, he ran a vast operation. Although his pictures of the Falls are spectacular, he is better known for his views of the exploration and settlement of the American West.

In this albumen print, made in the 1890s, Jackson captured both the power and the mystique of the American Falls at the Cave of the Winds. The photograph was made on paper coated with albumen and salt and later sensitized by the photographer.

This photograph of the Maid of the Mist, *caught between the cataracts, was made by the new Photochrome printing process, which Jackson acquired exclusively in 1896. His photos could now be accurately coloured for reproduction in quantity.*

The tourists move in

Before the railway age, the vast infrastructure of hotels, packaged tours, and sightseeing buses that we call tourism didn't exist in any organized fashion. But by 1860, when this photo was taken, the tourist industry at Niagara was in full bloom. Anyone stepping off the Great Western would immediately be importuned by a hack driver like this one to go to his favoured hotel (which paid him a commission) and to see all the sights along the gorge. The early railways brought in 50,000 people each summer. Today, 12 million visitors pour in. Most arrive by car.

It is not so easy today to contemplate the Falls in quiet seclusion.
But some manage to shut out the madding crowd. In 1859,
when William England made the double photograph above for the London
Stereoscopic Company, a solitary perch was easier to come by.

The young women drinking in the view of the Horseshoe Falls from
behind the railing on Goat Island, USA, are dressed in the height
of fashion in this 1906 stereoscopic photo. Today's dress is informal,
as are attitudes. In 1906, young people did not slouch.

In September 1860, the Prince of Wales arrived at Niagara with
his entourage, eager to see the great Blondin perform on the tightrope
over the gorge. What a starchy, silk-hatted, all-male company it was!
Today you may see bandannas at the Falls, but no toppers.

There was a time when only wealthy families could afford
to visit the Falls, the women arrayed in fashionable crinolines,
the men in starched wing collars. Today, families from all over
the world are just as fashionable in T-shirts and jeans.

Twelve million tourists–100 million snapshots

If every family of four that visits Niagara takes one roll of 35-millimetre film containing the usual 36 exposures, the figure quoted above is no exaggeration. Has anyone ever come to the Falls without a camera? Has anyone managed to escape without finishing at least one roll? At Niagara Falls, the cameras click as everyone is asked to watch the birdie.

How many wedding albums
are created at the Falls?
The so-called "honeymoon
capital of the world,"
Niagara has long been
a place for lovers and a
setting for nuptials. Why?
For the good reason that it
is cheap, easy to reach,
and eager to cater to
newlyweds. "Honeylunacy,"
as it used to be called,
did not exist before the
railway age. The earlier
"wedding trip" of the well-
to-do, on which the bride
and groom were accompanied
by a host of friends and
relatives, then gave way
to the more intimate honeymoon. Niagara Falls was
their destination because,
like Everest, it was there.

Romance has become less formal in the eighty-five-year period that separates the photographs on this page. Back in 1858, personal emotions were held in check. No young woman would have dared ruffle her beau's hair, at least not in public. In those days it was proper to conceal the female form from vulgar glances. Both the women and the men in their Prince Albert coats would have been shocked by the casual dress shown on the right. Only the wedding gown hints at a more formal age.

Therc was a time when
visitors were so mesmerized
by the cataract
that some tumbled over the edge.

That explains the guard rail.

On raucous Clifton Hill, the carnival never ends

Clowns, banners, daredevils, and spookery bring out the child in everyone. Blondin's effigy, teetering on the tightrope, emphasizes the long-standing role of the Falls as backdrop for theatrical high-jinks.

Clifton Hill is the modern counterpart of the nineteenth century's notorious "Front," the exuberant strip that stretched along the lip of the gorge from Table Rock to the Clifton House (now the site of the Oakes Garden Theatre). There, every kind of tout, blackguard, salesman, entrepreneur, and confidence man mulcted gullible travellers, who were far less sophisticated than today's tourists. The old Front is long gone, thanks to an active preservation movement that created Queen Victoria Park. But, set back from the Falls, the carnival goes on–more respectable than its predecessor but just as gaudy. Clifton Hill is its main artery, a neon thoroughfare where honeymoon hotels, souvenir shops, wax museums, and a cluster of attractions lure those visitors, who, for the moment at least, want some respite from the cascading waters and swirling mists. Like the tourists of a century past, you can have your photograph taken here, but without the danger of physical assault. Secure in your fake barrel or balloon you can prove that you've been to Niagara Falls.

Although real balloons sometimes soar over the Falls and helicopter rides are available every day, most tourists opt for a simulated experience. 'Twas ever thus. A century ago young ladies often preferred to be pictured against a painted backdrop instead of the real thing.

Tourists flock to see the barrel that took Annie Taylor—the first to perform the feat—over the Falls. In fact, it's a replica, and Annie bore little resemblance to this model. She was older and heavier, but her initiative brought her immortality.

Anyone who tries to go over the Falls in a barrel today faces a $5,000 fine. But if you can't experience the real thing you can still take home a souvenir photo. Customers are encouraged to feign fear, excitement, and the thrill of danger.

By day  **or by night**

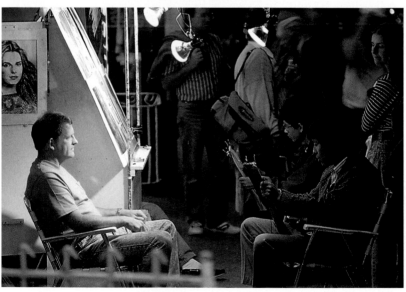

*Since the early 1950s, Clifton Hill shops
have been spilling over into side alleys and
adjoining lots, offering anything from a
souvenir totem to a hand-drawn portrait.*

"The Hill" never sleeps

Back in the early days, the cataract itself
provoked enough Gothic thrills to satisfy
the traveller. Now gargoyles, grottoes, and
tattooed ladies vie with it for attention.

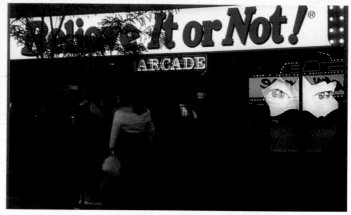

The Falls: Then and Now

Touring Niagara in the nineteenth century

Sightseeing at the Falls began in the 1820s, following the War of 1812. By then professional guides, such as Samuel Hooker, were taking visitors to the main points of interest. As early as 1840, 25,000 summer tourists were arriving. By 1846, that number had doubled. That was the year the first *Maid of the Mist* went into operation and the water-powered inclined railway was completed to take sightseers down to the boat landing at the base of the American Falls. The stream of tourists turned into a flood after 1855 when the first railway suspension bridge was completed, making possible a continuous tour of both sides of the gorge by carriage.

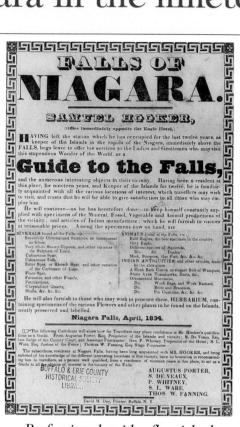

Professional guides flourished after the War of 1812. Since 1846 there have been ten Maids.

The major points of interest on the early tour were Table Rock, the vast platform of dolostone that overlooked the Horseshoe Falls; the Front, a noisy carnival stretched along the Canadian side of the gorge; and the Clifton House, then the premier watering place in Niagara. The suspension bridge itself was a sightseer's dream. On the American side, Prospect Point gave visitors the best overall view of both falls. Not far away, a wooden bridge took them across to the unspoiled glades of Goat Island. Another walkway led to the famous Terrapin Tower, built in 1833 on the turtle-shaped rocks at the very brink of the Horseshoe Falls.

*This is how Table Rock looked in 1829 when
William Bennett painted it from below. More than an acre in size,
it was the prime vantage point before it collapsed in 1850.*

Painted by W.J.Bennett.

Engraved, Printed & Coloured by J.Hill.

In the 1820s, the Porter brothers, who owned Goat Island, built a shaky pier extending 300 yards from the main island out to a series of half-submerged outcrops known as the Terrapin Rocks. It can be seen in the middle distance of this 1833 print. That year, a 45-foot lighthouse-shaped structure was built on the rock. It soon became a popular spot for sightseers.

*When William Bartlett visited the Falls in 1836,
the causeway leading to the tower was still terrifyingly
primitive. It was soon replaced by a sturdier structure.*

*Anna Jameson, the British art critic, found the Terrapin Tower
"detestably impudent... a puny monument of bad taste."
But Caroline Gilman, a Boston poet, was enchanted
by the breathtaking view–"the crown and glory of the whole."*

*For almost half a century
the world beat a path to
the tower before it faced
erosion and was demolished.
This early photograph shows
a group of Chinese visitors
experiencing the walkway.*

The American Falls, viewed from an overhang that served as a vantage point in 1848

In 1848, fashionable sightseers enjoyed a spectacular view of the rapids at Goat Island.

*In 1855, the pleasure park at
Prospect Point on the American side
was one of the most popular
spots on the Falls tour. Of course,
there was an admission fee.
Note the photographer's kiosk
in the background.*

*By 1900, when Niagara's attractions had
become world famous, a trip on the* Maid
of the Mist *was a must for tourists.*

Niagara — Entrance to Cave of Winds

(28) Looking at the tumbling, foaming waters, below the Falls, Niagara, U. S. A.
Copyright 1901 by Underwood & Underwood.

The spectacular Cave of the Winds (ABOVE)
and the fury of the Whirlpool Rapids (BELOW)
were high points on the tour.

The world's first railway suspension bridge becomes a sightseer's mecca

The town of Clifton got its first railway station in 1855 after the gorge was bridged. Niagara Falls now became the best-known tourist magnet in North America. For the first time, visitors could travel from the Canadian to the American side by foot, by carriage, or by steam train.

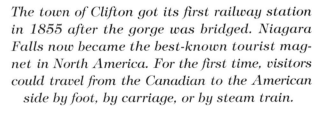

The railway bridge itself became a stop on the tour. Hanging across the gorge on ten-inch cables suspended from tall towers, it became a focal point for both artists and photographers. The view from the upper deck was also spectacular.

Roebling, the Ironmaster, builds a bridge to last

From 1855 to 1897, John Roebling's railway suspension bridge was one of the high points on the Niagara tour. Similar bridges crumpled, but when this bridge was finally retired to make way for a wider structure, its cables were as sound as when they were installed. Engineers scoffed at Roebling's design, but the Ironmaster, as he was called, knew what he was about. Rather than let the bridge sway (and twist in the wind), Roebling stiffened the two-tiered structure until it resembled a gigantic iron girder. It was actually an oblong metal box: railway tracks and a pedestrian walk ran along the top; wheeled traffic used the plank roadway at the bottom. In between was a massive nest of trusses, girders, and cables. A resolute German immigrant, Roebling founded the American wire rope industry, hence his knowledge of bridge cables. In 1869, while at work on the Brooklyn Bridge, he suffered the injury that killed him.

The plank roadway under the box-like bridge

. . . and the tour spans the gorge

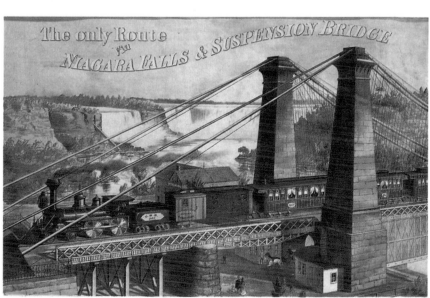

An unknown American folk artist painted this impression of Roebling's bridge, based on a professional canvas by Ferdinand Richardt. The poster shows the upper tier of the bridge and boasts that the Great Western Route is the only one to take sightseers over the gorge. It was on this bridge that crowds gathered to watch the great Blondin and his successors defy Niagara on tightropes.

Fun along the Great Gorge Route

The Great Gorge Route, established around the turn of the century, has been called "the most delightful street-car ride in the world." The passengers could climb aboard at any point on the route, which took them through the grass, flowers, and shrubbery of Queen Victoria Park, then along the edge of the cliff to the Whirlpool and on to Queenston, where it crossed on the Queenston-Lewiston bridge and descended to river level. Here sightseers were rewarded with a magnificent view of the Whirlpool and rapids, this time at close quarters. The trolleys then ascended the long, graded rise to the village of Niagara Falls, New York, returning to the Canadian side by the Upper Steel Arch (Honeymoon) Bridge. The route was so popular that one man, contemplating suicide, bought a ticket and enjoyed the trip before taking the fatal plunge. *At right,* the inclined railway that took tourists to the boat landing at the water's edge by the base of the American Falls.

. . . and frolic on Goat Island

Niagara—Follow the Leader, Goat Island.

Burlesque stereo cards enjoyed a brisk sale.

Peeping Toms posing on Goat Island: the card reads, "Have a look. You will have to hurry."

Another popular stereo card exploited Niagara's reputation as the world's honeymoon capital.

The Monteagle Hotel sprang up on the American side to take advantage of the bridge traffic.

Omnibuses waited at the suspension bridge to bring visitors to the Cataract House.

POWER

To the engineers and scientists who contemplated, in the late nineteenth century, the surging waters of Niagara, it seemed almost shameful that this stupendous 170-foot drop should be nothing more than an attraction for the rubbernecks to gaze upon. Although the French had operated a mill on the Niagara as early as 1758, the real breakthrough did not come until the age of electricity. Then, in 1893, the Columbian Exposition was lit entirely by hydro-electric power. As new electric companies began to spring up on both sides of the border, it became clear that the great cataract was threatened as a tourist attraction. Today, under an international agreement, only half its water is available for power during the summer. In the winter, when only a few tourists visit the Falls, the hydro plants can use up to 75 percent of the available water. But only the most eagle-eyed of visitors can perceive the Falls' diminished flow.

Four pioneers of hydro power

Edward Dean Adams

He was president of Cataract Construction, a New York firm organized to harness the power of the Falls. A financial wizard who had just rescued a railroad from bankruptcy, he took a daring gamble in 1890 when his company began to bore a two-mile tunnel, 160 feet under the village of Niagara Falls, New York. The tunnel was designed as a tailrace to carry water from a point above the Falls and return it to the river, once it had been used to drive machinery. But what kind of machinery? And how would the power be transmitted? By belts, shafts, or cables? By compressed air? Or by the latest scientific marvel, electricity? Adams started the tunnel without having the answers. He launched an international competition to determine the best methods. The results were mixed, but in the end electricity won. Water-powered wheels at the base of a deep shaft drove the turbines in the new powerhouse, which was, appropriately, named in honour of Adams himself.

Jacob Schoellkopf

He was a self-made man with a history of buying up bankrupt tanneries and making them pay. One day in 1877 he bid on a bankrupt, unfinished "hydraulic canal" at the Falls and got it, with the land and water rights, for $71,000. That night he went back to Buffalo to tell his wife. "Momma, I bought the ditch," was the way he put it. She was not entranced, nor was his partner in the milling business. "What'll you do with all that water, Jacob? You can't use it and you can't sell it." But Schoellkopf finished the canal, and by 1882, several industries were using its power, generated by turbines that operated machinery through belts and pulleys. Schoellkopf quickly saw the potential of electricity and built a small powerhouse on the canal to operate street lamps in the village. Soon he had built a second and was rivalling the Adams operation. In 1918 the Schoellkopf company was merged with Adams's Niagara Falls Power.

Adam Beck

A cigar-box manufacturer who became mayor of London, Ontario, he was the spark-plug behind the campaign for public power in the province at the century's turn. As a Conservative cabinet minister, following the election of 1905, he headed a commission of inquiry into electrical power, then in the hands of private entrepreneurs. This led, after a brisk campaign, to the creation in 1906 of the Hydro-Electric Power Commission of Ontario, with Beck as its hard-driving chairman. By 1914 he determined to build an enormous hydro-electric plant on the Niagara River. He managed to conceal its real cost from the provincial government while waging a titanic battle against Sir William Mackenzie, the forceful head of the Toronto Power Company, the largest private power enterprise on the Canadian side. Mackenzie finally sold out, and public power was victorious. Both hydro plants at Niagara are named for Adam Beck.

Robert Moses

Like Adam Beck, Robert Moses
was known on his home turf as
a man who got things done. More
than any other, he had shaped
New York City and much of New
York State, building bridges,
expressways, and parks, often
by bulldozing all opposition. He
was Governor Tom Dewey's
obvious choice as energy czar,
charged with building a huge new
powerplant on the American
side of the Niagara River.
Political squabbling held up
the job for eight years. (In the
meantime Ontario began and
completed Beck 2 across the
river.) Moses also found himself
in an unseemly battle with the
Tuscarora Indians, who didn't
want him to take a big chunk of
their reservation for a reservoir.
Moses was obliged to settle for
much less than he wanted, but
once the haggling was over, he
finished the job. Moses was less
interested in the powerplant
than in the parkway he built along
the Niagara gorge. Both plant
and parkway now bear his name.

Nikola Tesla

In the 1890s he was the most celebrated
scientist on earth, the Serbian genius who
made the long-distance transmission of
Niagara Falls power possible through
the use of alternating current. He
worked that out in his head while reciting
Goethe's *Faust* during a stroll through
a Budapest park. His photographic
memory made it unnecessary for him to
draw a blueprint or write anything down.
He "saw" his inventions in his mind.
Incredibly sensitive (he could hear a
watch ticking three rooms away), he
could speak eight languages without an
accent. His interest in the potential of
water power began in childhood. In
America he worked briefly for Thomas
Edison, but the inventor scorned his
theories. George Westinghouse was
more farsighted. He bought up Tesla's
patents, won the "Battle of the Currents,"
and gained the contract to light the 1893
Columbian Exposition. Today the *tesla*,
a unit of magnetic induction, honours the
name of the man who made it all possible.

When powerhouses looked like palaces

The two powerhouses shown here, one American, one Canadian, represent the high point of industrial architecture in North America. The main stairway of the office building at the Edward Dean Adams powerplant on the American side could grace the rotunda of a grand hotel or an Italian palazzo. Adams was determined to go first class and hired Stanford White, the prominent New York architect, to produce a building that, Adams said, must be "artistic in grandeur, dignified, impressive, enduring."

The Italianate exterior of the Toronto Power Company's station was the design of Edward Lennox, the architect who also planned the Old City Hall in Toronto. Lennox was a friend of Sir Henry Pellatt, one of the trio of industrialists who built the plant. Later, for Sir Henry, Lennox built Toronto's famous palace, the turreted Casa Loma.

824
6-25-00 WHEELPIT LOOKING NORTH.

Hacking out a wheel pit for the first powerplant

The first major attempt to use the power locked up in the Falls was made on the American side. Here, the half-completed wheel pit of the Adams powerplant, cut from the unyielding rock of the Niagara Escarpment, is shown in a photograph made on June 25, 1900. The pit, when completed, was 160 feet deep, slightly less than the height of the American Falls. Water taken from the river just above the cataract dropped to the base of the pit, where it drove the great turbines used to produce the electrical power that turned the town of Niagara Falls, New York, into a thriving industrial city. Companies that required huge amounts of power relocated at Niagara. Once the water did its job, it was carried to a down-river spillway by a vast tunnel bored under the town itself. The elegant Adams powerplant was built directly above this wheel pit.

948
2-2700 CHAINING ROCK INTO BO... SLE WAY.

The real problem facing the hydro pioneers was the huge quantity of water needed to run the turbines. How to get rid of it? The only answer was to build tunnels running from the wheel pits to a point below the Falls. The Americans actually began to build their tunnel under the town of Niagara Falls even before they knew whether or not hydro-electric power would be produced. The tunnel is shown above as it looked in July 1895. The tunnel for Toronto Power is shown below during construction in 1904. The size of these tunnels gives some idea of the amounts of water used.

LEFT
Six months after the photo on the previous page was taken, the great wheel pit was much deeper. Rock slabs chained to boxes were removed by cableway.

LEFT
The second Ontario Hydro powerplant to be named for Adam Beck was then the world's largest. Here workmen pour the first concrete into penstock trenches. The date is April 29, 1952.

RIGHT
Dwarfed by their surroundings, scalers begin clean-up operations at the north abutment of the Robert Moses powerplant, March 7, 1961. The huge project produced more electrical power than both Beck plants combined.

A river encased in concrete

Facing each other across the Niagara are two of the greatest power facilities in the world: Adam Beck 1 and 2 on the Canadian side (LEFT) and the gigantic Robert Moses station on the American. Together the three plants produce more than 31.5 million kW, fuelling the industrial heartland in the northeastern quarter of North America.

Residents of Niagara Falls, Ontario, faced a steep climb of
350 steps as they inspected the interior of the first of two
tunnels, each five and a half miles long. These tunnels now
carry one-fifth of all the water of the Niagara River directly beneath the Canadian community to the Beck 2 plant
farther down river. Some of the water goes into a storage
reservoir at the plant, to be used when the need arises.

The Falls today: towers, tunnels, and jet boats

From a glassed-in viewing tower 500 feet above the Horseshoe Falls, modern tourists look down on the continent's great natural wonder. In earlier times, visitors viewed the Falls from Table Rock, a huge slab of dolostone just a few feet from the lip of the Horseshoe. But like the other famous landmarks, Table Rock is long gone. New attractions have replaced older ones. Visitors can go "behind the sheet" protected from the blast of the cataract by tunnels bored into the rock. They get a better view of the Whirlpool from the Spanish Aero Car. And jet boats provide a thrill only a hardy few were willing to hazard in the old days.

After a century and a half the *Maid*s still take visitors into the blinding spray

Linking past and present, the little *Maid of the Mist* remains one of the primary attractions at Niagara–an experience that few can forget. Protected from the lashing spray by modern plastic coats, passengers can gaze up at the furious waters, as Charles Dickens once did from a ferry, "deafened by the noise, half blinded by the spray" but no longer soaked to the skin.

So popular has the boat journey become that four Maids are needed to handle the crowds. BELOW: On land and on water, visitors are drenched by the clouds of spray at the spectacular Cave of the Winds.

At the
Cave of the Winds,
the lash of Niagara's
spray never abates

In the early days, visitors clambered down the slopes of the gorge to visit the Cave of the Winds off Goat Island. Now a modern elevator assists them. The actual cave has been worn away by the river's ceaseless erosion, but a series of wooden staircases and platforms has been constructed so that today's tourists, in yellow slickers, can experience in safety and relative comfort the age-old fury of the Falls.

Looking down on the Whirlpool

From balloons, towers, helicopters, and devices such as the one shown here, tourists today are given a view of Niagara not available in earlier times. Suspended in the Spanish Aero Car, high above the Whirlpool, passengers focus their cameras on the maelstrom below. Designed in Spain, the car has been operating since 1916.

On Goat Island, a little bit of yesterday

Goat Island, on the American side, has been called "the noblest of nature's gardens." Its luxuriant vegetation could not exist without the spray from the Falls, which has created a natural nursery for every kind of indigenous wildflower, shrub, and shade tree.

When Augustus Porter bought the island, back in 1816, he resolved to leave it alone and undisturbed. As a result, there are still corners on the island that look and even feel as they did in his day. Here, one seems to have travelled back beyond the hurly-burly of our time.

Jet craft zoom where barrels once bobbed

*In the old days, only a handful of daredevils
was bold enough to try to navigate the Niagara gorge.
Today, in computer-controlled jet boats, the trip is thrilling
but entirely safe.*

A battered scow becomes
a tourist attraction

*Every tourist wants to hear
the story of this big steel
scow, which has been stuck
fast in the current just above
the Falls since 1918. The two
men aboard were saved from
certain death by Red Hill, Sr.
Though invalided home with
war wounds, Hill went out on
a rope, hand over hand, to
untangle the breeches-buoy
that brought the two to safety*

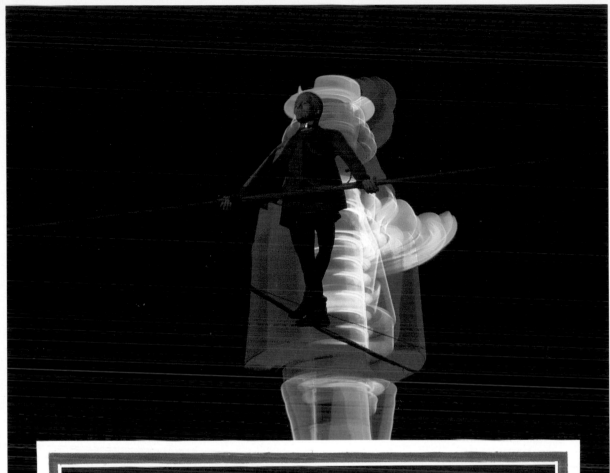

The Drama of the Falls

No greater cyclorama has ever existed than the cascading background of Niagara. Before it, a variety of showpeople—some professional, some amateur—have worked their individual magic. In winter and in summer, the Falls have provided a natural backdrop against which the gamut of human drama has been played. For two centuries every kind of entrepreneur, commercial as well as theatrical, has seen the Falls as a wonder to be profitably exploited as well as admired.

3631.

Strong men pale and ladies swoon as the Prince of Manila takes his ease high above Niagara's gorge

Strong men were always turning pale and ladies forever swooning in nineteenth-century accounts of daredevilry, but there's no doubt that the great Blondin did cause hearts to palpitate as he danced, skipped, minced, strutted, and even somersaulted on a 2,000-foot-long, three-inch Manila rope, stretched 160 feet above the boiling chasm. Some 25,000 spectators poured into Niagara to see the Prince of Manila in his pink tights cavort on the rope–hanging from it by one leg, performing handstands, lying full length on it, crossing blindfold in a sack, pushing a wheelbarrow, balancing on a chair above sudden death. On August 17, 1859, before an audience of 40,000, he carried his manager, Harry Colcord, across on his back, a considerable feat since his total load, including the balancing pole, weighed close to 200 pounds. When he cooked omelets on a small stove and lowered them on a cord to the *Maid of the Mist*, passengers fought for pieces, hoping, perhaps, that they might ingest something of Blondin's daring.

*A spider's web of guys steadies
Blondin's swaying rope as he carries
Colcord across, piggyback.*

THE CHAMPION, Jean François Gravelet, a.k.a. Blondin, was so popular that special music was composed to honour his feats. By the time Blondin reached Niagara, he had made the horizontal tightrope his own. (Earlier acrobats had either used the slackwire or mounted a tightrope fastened diagonally from a height to an attachment fixed in the ground.) Blondin had been rope walking since the age of five. He became a professional at nine, the year he was orphaned – a prodigy without a rival. At twenty-seven, he joined the French Ravel troupe of performers on their tour of North America. That led to a visit to the Falls. "What a splendid place to bridge with a tightrope," he remarked in 1858. His friends thought he was joking, but he was deadly serious, as he demonstrated the following summer.

meets his match

Farini hangs by his knees above the flood. Later he brought a washer to launder ladies' hankies.

THE CHALLENGER, Bill Hunt of Port Hope, a.k.a. Signor Guillermo Antonio Farini, saw Blondin perform at Niagara in the early summer of 1860 and announced that he would duplicate all of his feats. Few believed him, but by August he was doing just that. His many stunts included a descent by a 200-foot rope to the *Maid of the Mist* and a terrifying and exhausting climb back up to the slackwire to complete the journey. A better businessman than Blondin, he hired four excursion boats to bring in paying customers who coughed up fifty cents apiece for reserved seats. Farini's later career was wide ranging. Horticulturist, explorer, inventor, painter, sculptor, impresario, he is said to have been the model for Du Maurier's Svengali. Farini, who shot a woman from a cannon on the London stage, certainly looks the part in the engraving above.

A gaggle of rope
dancers helps create
the Niagara legend

Clifford Calverly,
*the last of the big-time
funambulists, wowed the crowd
in the 1890s when he propelled
a wheelbarrow of his own design
across on his swaying cable.*

*Calverly established a speed
record on one crossing by
rushing from bank to bank in a
fraction over 2 minutes, 45
seconds. Of 15 rope walkers, only
Stephen Peer fell to his death.*

"Professor" J. F. Jenkins
*crossed in 1869 on a kind of velocipede,
which, being fastened to the rope,
was in no danger of toppling.*

Signor Bellini,
*the "Australian Blondin," in 1873 plunged into
the furious river from an India-rubber rope
attached to the main cable.*

Marie Spelterina,
*a circus performer, was the only woman
to cross the gorge on a tightrope.
She did it wearing peach baskets on her feet.*

Samuel John Dixon,
*a Toronto photographer whose hobby
was wire walking, crossed in 1890 and 1891
but realized only $56 for his feats.*

The barrel riders grab the limelight

The weedy man on the right is Carlisle Graham, the "Hero of Whirlpool Rapids," a cooper who made four trips through those waters beginning in 1886. In 1889 he claimed to have gone over the Falls in his barrel, a boast that was quickly exposed as a fraud. Later, he announced that he and Martha Wagenfuhrer, shown below, would ride tandem barrels over the American Falls, but that too was only a boast. Martha borrowed Graham's barrel in 1891 and successfully navigated the Whirlpool, an adventure that gained her a fat contract on the vaudeville circuit. Her friend Maud Willard, a burlesque performer, attempted the feat a day later and suffocated. Both women were emulating Sadie Allen, who in 1886 challenged the Whirlpool on a dare and emerged alive.

GRAHAM,
The Hero of Whirlpool Rapids, and his Barrel.

Martha Wagenfuhrer

GRAHAM,
THE HERO OF WHIRLPOOL RAPIDS AND HIS BARREL.

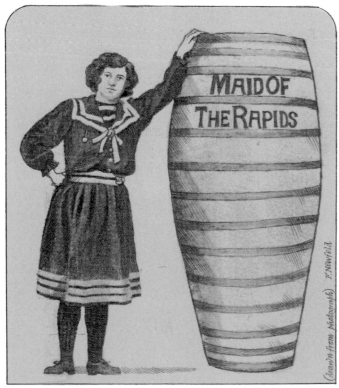

Maud Willard

Sadie Allen with partner, George Hazlett

Annie Taylor takes the big plunge and puts her rivals in the shade

On October 24, 1901, Annie Edson Taylor, a bulky woman of 63, made history when she became the first human being to plunge over the Horseshoe Falls, and in a barrel of her own design. That feat immortalized her, at least in the Clifton Hill side-shows, as the spurious likeness shown here demonstrates. Annie, who claimed to be only 42, did it for the money. Alas, rich profits failed to materialize, partly because Annie shrank from making the dime museum appearances her manager urged upon her. She herself was a dancing teacher who had lost most of her business to prettier and slimmer rivals. Bad luck kept dogging her.

Her battered barrel was stolen after she made her plunge. (The cat, allegedly used to test the barrel, was also spurious.) For the rest of her life she was a prisoner of her own exploits, as she tried to make a living based on fading memories of her famous feat. Hack drivers pointed her out to tourists on the street, a pathetic figure, wrinkled and half blind, still proudly posing with her new barrel. Yet one can only admire her. In an era when few women had public status she was a bold entrepreneur. As she said, "I've done what no other woman in the world had nerve to do." Her major mistake was to pretend she was younger than she looked. Had she lied with more wit and said she was 75, the world might have taken some notice. She died at 83, insisting that she was only 57! The barrel ride, she said, had prematurely aged her.

Bobby Leach, a roistering, British-born saloonkeeper, was everything Annie was not. A hard-drinking pool shark and a spinner of yarns, he became, in 1911, the second human to go over the Falls in a barrel. Annie wanted nothing to do with him and pleaded with the press not to associate her name with his "in any way, shape, or manner." Leach himself died of complications after slipping on an orange peel during a New Zealand tour.

A tranquil start, a harrowing finish

*Annie Taylor is shown above before she discreetly
removed her outer clothing and entered the barrel.*

OPPOSITE:
*The end of her short, turbulent voyage.
Carlisle Graham (LEFT) helps her ashore as Red Hill, Sr.,
Niagara's most famous riverman, extends a helping hand.*

Red Hill, Sr., whose obsession was the Niagara River,
won four life-saving medals. His feats were listed on his famous
barrel, which Red, Jr., rides in the photograph below.
But the senior Hill never took the barrel over the Falls.

The Hill family legend ends in tragedy

Red Hill, Jr., emulated his father and wanted to surpass him. Lacking funds to build a proper barrel, he settled for a contraption of inner tubes known as the Thing. He made the plunge on August 5, 1950, and died in a tangle of rubber tubes and netting.

William Fitzgerald, who hurtled over the Falls in his Plunge-O-Sphere in July 1961, was not a typical daredevil. He wasn't interested in profit or publicity. Indeed, he made the trip under the assumed name Nathan Boya. Why did he invest his life savings in a stunt he refused to discuss? To this day he has never given any explanation. In fact, he has stubbornly denied the various theories others have advanced to explain his feat.

On October 5, 1985, John David Munday became the first Canadian to plunge over the Falls and live. A 48-year-old diesel mechanic and garage owner from Caistor Centre, Ontario, he was the seventh person to survive the attempt. The Niagara Falls police frown on such escapades, and the Munday crew tried for weeks to elude them. Finally Munday, a veteran of 1,400 parachute jumps, gave the police the slip and satisfied his persistent obsession to conquer the cataract by barrel.

Roger Woodward, aged seven, wearing nothing more than a life jacket and trunks, survived an accidental drop over the Horseshoe Falls in July 1960. Hurled from a small boat after its motor failed, he and an adult friend were carried over the crest of the cataract. Only Roger survived. (His sister, Deanne, was pulled from the river at the last moment.) The experience helped change his life. Years later, after pondering the reason for his existence, Roger Woodward became a committed evangelist.

Exploiting the drama

A Buffalo artist's portrayal of a Niagara water nymph enlivened a poster promoting the Pan-American Exposition of 1901.

The commercialization of the Falls began in the 1850s when Thomas Barnett's museum and a troop of tightrope walkers brought in the tourists. But the Falls did not become a commercial icon until the next century, when their image was used to promote everything from footwear to breakfast cereal, as the pictures on the following pages show.

Back in 1834 wallpaper, often depicting scenery, was all the rage. The Falls were naturally a subject.

Painted for the Niagara Mohawk powerplant, this oil was intended to demonstrate the awesome horsepower available from the Falls.

In 1986, Philippe Petit repeated Blondin's triumph for the huge screen of the IMAX theatre at the Falls.

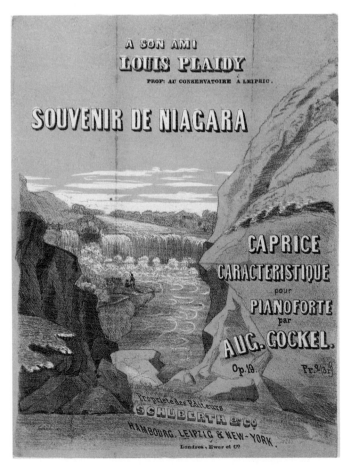

LEFT
This mural at the Schoellkopf powerplant was entitled The Birth of Power. The artist was the fashionable Willy Pogany.

RIGHT
In the days before radio and television, sheet music sales soared, including this song based on Niagara.

The Home of
SHREDDED WHEAT

NIAGARA FALLS
NEW YORK

The Cleanest, Finest, Most
Hygienic Food Factory
in the World

In this beautiful, sunlit bakery are baked every day in the year two
million Shredded Wheat Biscuits, made of the whole wheat, nothing
added, nothing taken away. Deliciously nourishing, wholesome and
strengthening. Try them for breakfast.

W.M. LAIRD'S   Elegant Footwear

NIAGARA FALLS

*The best way to
sell a breakfast
cereal was to
locate the plant
at Niagara Falls,
New York, and
use the icon on
each box of
Shredded Wheat.*

*Even shoe
manufacturers
employed the
image to peddle
footwear.*

OPPOSITE
*Marilyn Monroe
was not yet
a star when
this picture was
made. But the
name "Niagara"
had a potent
sales appeal.*

The ravages of nature

For sheer drama, no human daredevil risking his life on a tightrope or in a barrel has been able to compete with the savage forces of nature that continue to make their mark on Niagara's gorge and on the Falls itself. The famous Honeymoon Bridge, stretched across the frozen river like a broken serpent in January 1938, demonstrates man's impotence in the face of natural calamity. No human endeavour could have saved the structure from the ice jam–any more than it could have saved the Schoellkopf powerplant or Prospect Point from the erosion that has forced the Falls seven miles upstream in the 12,500 years of their existence. In spite of monumental efforts, the bridge was clearly doomed by the worst ice jam in 30 years. The ice climbed 75 feet up the bank, virtually smothering the Ontario Power Company's plant. Work crews toiled for 48 hours trying to save the bridge as the ice pressed against its abutments. At 4.15 p.m., January 28, the end came with a loud crackle and a low rumble. In just five seconds the bridge settled into the gorge. It lay there on the ice for 74 days before it vanished beneath the rotting surface with monstrous splashes, swallowed up in pieces by the river, while onlookers gasped. Its replacement, the Rainbow Bridge, was rushed to completion by November 1941.

The end of the Honeymoon

From January 28, 1938, when it collapsed (OPPOSITE),
until April 12, when a chunk fell through the ice and
the rest drifted downstream to sink beneath the
waters (BELOW), the broken bridge was the greatest
tourist attraction in Niagara, rivalling the Falls.

The collapse of Prospect Point

On July 8, 1954, as thousands watched from behind a
protective fence, 185,000 tons of rock, comprising most
of Prospect Point, crashed into the gorge with a mighty
roar. The ceaseless erosion had eliminated the most
famous vantage point on the American side and also
carved a great wedge-shaped section out of the American Falls, altering the crest line. For eons, water seep-
ing through the crevices in the soft shale, alternately
freezing and thawing, had forced ever-widening rifts
in the rock. Nothing could have prevented the disaster.

A powerplant is doomed

At five o'clock on the afternoon of June 8, 1956, tourists strolling through Queen Victoria Park on the Canadian side of the gorge heard a strange noise coming from across the river–rumbling and grumbling at first, then a thunderous roar. They stared in disbelief at the cliff above the Schoellkopf powerplant on the water's edge. The top of the gorge began to shake, and for several moments it seemed that hundreds of tons of rock hung in the air as if suspended by wires. Then the entire mass–400 feet across, 40 feet thick–cascaded down, crushing the roof of the powerplant below. Once again man's handiwork had been the victim of the same erosive process that created Niagara Falls. To the workers inside the plant, it was as if a jet plane had taken off. They had been warned about the dangerous seepage in the cliff above. Now, as the plant's windows began to pop and the floor to heave alarmingly, they dashed for the exits. A huge crack opened in the end wall, widening to a two-foot gap before the building split open. The ceiling began to fall. Forty workmen raced for the door on the downstream side. One, Richard Draper, didn't make it. He was blown out of a window to his death. With two-thirds of the plant a twisted mass of steel, the U.S. power shortage grew worse. The disaster did help shatter the political roadblock delaying the massive Moses power project downriver. Finally, the Americans went ahead.

By the sixties, a series of massive rock falls that began in 1931 had created a mountain of broken rock in front of the American Falls. At some points, the pile was 100 feet high, obscuring the view of the falling water. Everything from small stones to boulders as big as houses lay in heaps outward for 50 feet from the precipice over which the water flowed. Unlike the more powerful Horseshoe Falls, the smaller cataract did not have enough force to remove the rock or the depth of water below to hide it. And so, with international approval, U.S. Army engineers carried out, in the summer of 1969, "the most exciting challenge in the history of Niagara Falls." They dried up the cataract for five months in order to find out what was causing the rock falls and to ascertain some method of stopping them. Workmen (LEFT) sprayed and sandblasted the dry riverbed to discover that the friable cliff was a labyrinth of passageways through which the water seeped, again freezing and melting to expand the cracks and weaken the shales. Could the erosion be halted? An international board, studying the findings, came to the reluctant conclusion that it shouldn't be. The 280,000 cubic yards of rubble were "a dynamic part of the natural condition of the Falls," it said. It was better, the board concluded, to let nature take its course.

OVERLEAF

A trickle of water pours over the broken cliff face of the American Falls, as engineers probe the fissures in the dried-up riverbed above. They found vast cavities hidden within the rock.

The drama of winter

Ninety percent of those who visit Niagara Falls do so in the summertime. Yet it can be argued that the most striking impressions are achieved when the great cataract is locked in a mantle of ice. Even though the flow in winter is smaller, the effect is spectacular, partly because the congealed spray cloaks every tree and railing in a thick garment of frost. The picture above was made about 1860, when photography was young and one-of-a-kind ambrotypes like this one were framed and mounted in hinged metal boxes to be carried as souvenirs in men's pockets or women's handbags. This photograph was made from the Canadian side, facing the American Falls, which, like the Niagara River, are not yet frozen. Soon an ice bridge will form, briefly linking Canada and the United States.

When the Falls freeze solid, Niagara becomes a fairyland

When an ice bridge forms, Niagara takes on a supernatural look. But this can happen only after several weeks of freezing weather have left the surface of Lake Erie covered by vast sheets of ice. If a thaw follows and the ice breaks up, high winds drive it into the Niagara, creating a river of floes racing relentlessly toward the Falls. Hour after hour the ice chunks hurtle over the Falls in a mighty frozen avalanche. Then, if the weather grows colder and more ice piles up, all the chunks are wedged together in a solid ice bridge— a labyrinth of hummocks and crevasses. The picture at left shows the Falls themselves frozen solid.
BELOW, one thrill seeker has scrambled to the peak of the largest hummock.

Fun seekers once defied danger to cavort on the great ice bridges

Before such activity was banned, the great ice bridges of the nineteenth century became the playground for hundreds of thrill seekers in winter. Such bridges did not always form, but in certain years, the ice stretched from shore to shore in a wild, rumpled mass. When the bridge was pronounced solid—when all the small chunks of ice hurled over the Falls had congealed into a craggy expanse of humps and clefts—men and women risked their lives in a race to be the first across. The timid gathered by the thousands on the shore or on the bridge overhead to follow these wild scrambles, whose winners were celebrated in the press. An informal winter carnival followed, the crowds on the ice singing, laughing, paying top prices for coffee and sandwiches, the cliffs echoing with their shouts. Men planted flags on hillocks to record they'd been the first to clamber to the top. Others explored crevasses to estimate the thickness of the ice. Some of these were 30 to 40 feet deep, suggesting that the ice itself, most of which was submerged, was more than 100 feet thick—strong enough, as it turned out, to bear the weight of a horse and carriage, until the break came.

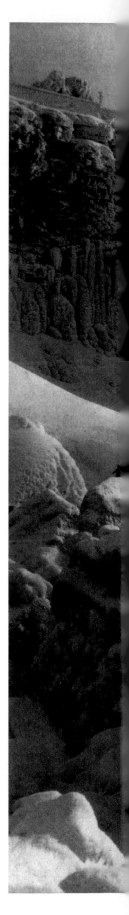

Ice palaces like this were once a Falls feature.

Natural caverns of ice formed beneath the Falls.

Making the best of winter

After the ice bridges formed, the Niagara River became a frozen no man's land between two nations. Small, temporary shacks sprang up selling everything from tintypes to bootleg whiskey, their owners safe in the knowledge that the geographical ambiguity of their position made police action impossible. But in 1912 tragedy struck. The ice bridge collapsed: three people drowned. All future ice bridges were declared out of bounds. Visitors must be content today to contemplate the drama of winter from the safety of the shore.

Photographer's shack on the ice lures visitors.

How one photographer views the Falls

The modern colour photographs appearing on these and previous pages were taken between May and December, 1992. Paul Casselman, a Toronto photographer, made more than a dozen trips to Niagara to capture the Falls in various moods. "All tourists find their way to the crest of the Falls," Casselman points out, "and they take a moment to commemorate the event with a snapshot or video camera. Often I'd volunteer to take the souvenir snap with their camera and then I'd take one with mine for this book. I like very much the informality and spontaneity of these photographs." A graduate of the Ontario College of Art and a contributor to major newspapers and magazines, Casselman has won several awards for his work.

Each summer,
the world comes
to Niagara

*As a photographer
who specializes in people,
Paul Casselman was
astonished and delighted
by the variety he
encountered at Niagara.*

The photo above of a young couple on Goat Island embracing in the rain is Casselman's favourite. "Oblivious to me, they kissed passionately, and I captured this moment of calm in the storm." Months later he returned to make the autumn study below.

There are very few spots left along the Niagara gorge that show how the region looked in the days before the white man came, but Casselman found this one. "While exploring the area, I climbed the steep embankment on the Canadian side and through a veil of branches caught a glimpse of the falls that suggested to me a time before the taming of Niagara."

159

"The plume of Niagara is magical, as it creates ethereal shapes in the early morning and fabulous rainbows in the late afternoon." It was this vision that early visitors found transcendental, conjuring up as it did ghostly apparitions rising to the heavens. There was something eerie about these misty pillars, seen from afar above the dark forest, and something godlike about the full-throated roar of the cataract booming in the distance.